Benjamin Britt

MW00452214

NOCTURNAL

Benjamin Britten

NOCTURNAL

after John Dowland

for Guitar

Op. 70

FABER **ff** MUSIC

Come, heavy Sleep, the image of true Death,

And close up these my weary weeping eyes,

Whose spring of tears doth stop my vital breath,

And tears my heart with Sorrow's sigh-swoll'n cries.

Come and possess my tired thought-worn soul,

That living dies, till thou on me be stole.

The right of Benjamin Britten to be identified as the composer of the musical work entitled Nocturnal after John Dowland *is hereby asserted. The name of Benjamin Britten as composer must therefore be stated in association with any performance, recording or other use of this work or any part of it. Any derogatory treatment of this work is illegal. No arrangement of this work may be made without the prior written permission of the publishers.*

Permission to perform this work in public must be obtained from the Society duly controlling performing rights unless there is a current licence for public performance from the Society in force in relation to the premises at which the performance is to take place. Such permission must be obtained in the UK from Performing Right Society Ltd, 29–33 Berners Street, London W1P 4AA.

© 1964, 1965 by Faber and Faber Ltd
Copyright assigned to Faber Music Ltd 1965
Published by Faber Music Ltd
3 Queen Square London WC1N 3AU
Music engraved by Novello and Co Ltd
Cover design by S & M Tucker
Printed in England by Caligraving Ltd
All rights reserved

ISBN 0-571-50005-6

To buy Faber Music publications or to find out about the full range of titles available please contact your local music retailer or Faber Music sales enquiries:

Faber Music Limited, Burnt Mill, Elizabeth Way, Harlow, CM20 2HX England Tel: +44 (0)1279 82 89 82   Fax: +44 (0)1279 82 89 83 sales@fabermusic.com   www.fabermusic.com

EDITOR'S NOTE

In view of the intricate character of this piece, I have endeavoured to finger it as succinctly as is compatible with the composer's original phrase marks, which are of course of great importance for the interpretation of the work.

Those intimate with the technicalities – and indeed difficulties – of phrasing in a convincing way upon the guitar will find that the dotted line thus: ⌣........⌣ (L.H. legato or slur) will not only lend support to the musical interpretation, but will also facilitate playing.

The song upon which this work is based in No.20 in *The First Book of Songs or Ayres of Four Parts* by John Dowland, published in 1597.

JULIAN BREAM

The first performance of *Nocturnal* was
given by Julian Bream at the Aldeburgh Festival
June 12th 1964

Duration: *c*.14 minutes

For Julian Bream

NOCTURNAL

Edited by Julian Bream

BENJAMIN BRITTEN
Op. 70

© 1964, 1965 by Faber and Faber Ltd
© 1965 by Faber Music Ltd

II Very agitated
(Molto agitato)

attacca

4

III Restless *(rubato: ♩.)*
(Inquieto)

IV Uneasy (*slow* ♩)
(*Ansioso*)

attacca

V March-like (♩)
(Quasi una Marcia)

singing (cantabile)

attacca

VI Dreaming (slow ♩)
(Sognante)

attacca

VII Gently rocking
(*Cullante*)

VIII Passacaglia (*measured*)
(*misurato*)

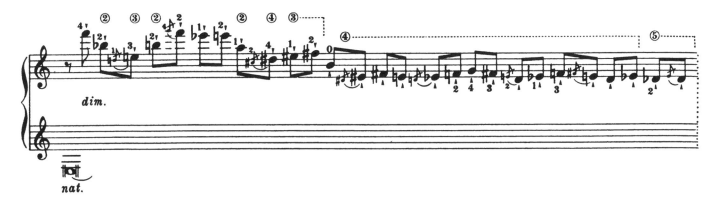

starting broadly (*cominciando largamente*)

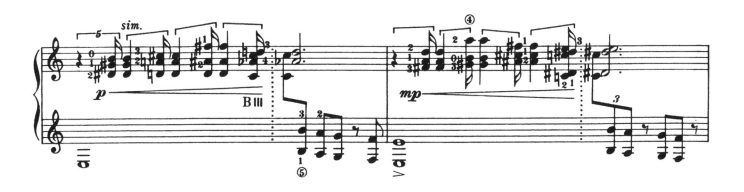

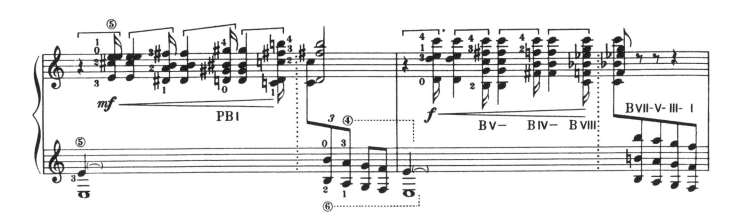

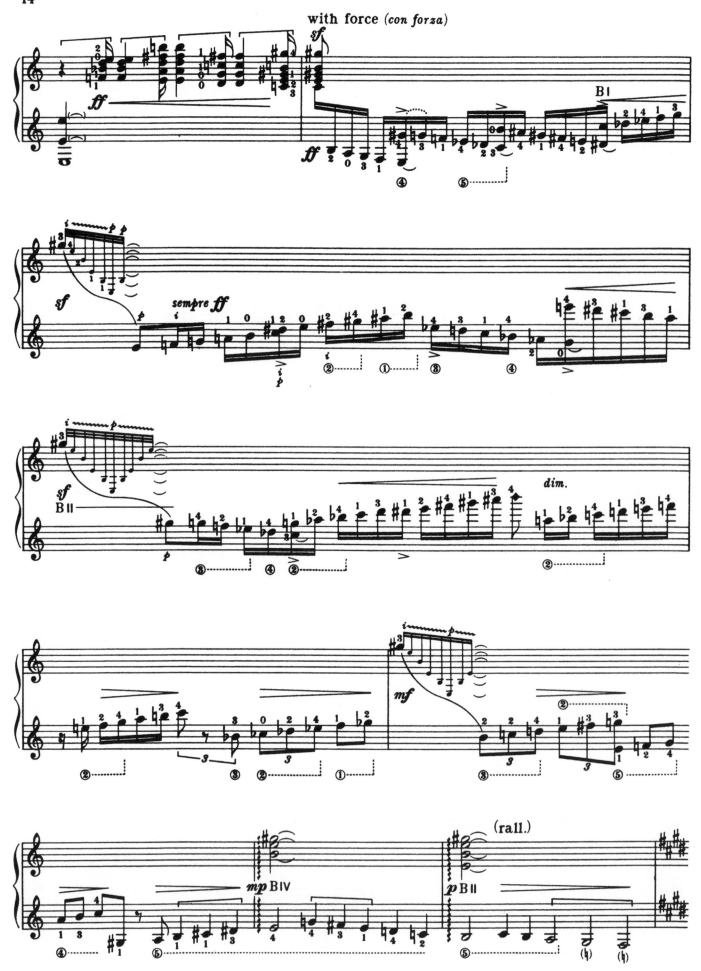

Slow and quiet *(Molto tranquillo)*

slower and dying away
(più lento e morendo)

as soft as possible
(quasi niente)

Aldeburgh- Nov. 11th, 1963.